Book Details and Benefits

- 69 High quality full colour sex vouchers.
- Contains a wide range of fun but filthy sexual challenges and prompts. (suitable for beginners to advanced)
- Each voucher has its own unique set of instructions printed on the back.
- Guaranteed to bring you closer together and inject some passion and excitement into your relationship.
- Contains 12 Blank vouchers which can be customised to suit your own fantasies and fetishes.
- We have included more than 1 voucher for some of our top voted challenges, so you can enjoy more than once.
- Some challenges are easy and others require a little bit of planning.

How to Use the Vouchers

- Cut along the guided lines to release the vouchers. This leaves a "stub" in the book.
- On the stub you can fill in information - Date voucher was redeemed? - Favourite part? - Rating from 1 - 10?
- Filling out details on the stub is optional, but it does give an insight into how you both felt about a challenge.
- I appreciate that people have different boundaries and preferences, so if you don't agree with a certain voucher please skip it and dont feel bad about it, we are all at different levels on our sexual journey.

Various Ways to Redeem the Vouchers

- Take it in turns to pick a voucher each. Once a week, once a month, it's your choice.
- Work through the book in order, from start to finish.
- Flick through the book without looking and select a random voucher each time.
- Or just pick a voucher you like and present it to your partner whenever you are feeling horny.

Lastly, thank you for you purchasing this booklet. I really hope it brings you both some joy and plenty of orgasms!

If you are brave enough feel free to use the insta / tiktok hashtag "#dirtyvouchers". When you are about to use a voucher or when you have completed one, along with your thoughts about it.

Thanks again.

GOOD LUCK AND ENJOY!

| DATE REDEEMED : |
| FAVOURITE PART : |
| RATING FROM 1 TO 10 : |
| VOUCHER NO : EREN1UCD |

THIS VOUCHER ENTITLES YOU TO ONE:

JUST THE TIP

SEX VOUCHER

REDEEMABLE ANYTIME
NO EXPIRY

VOUCHER NO : EREN1UCD

| DATE REDEEMED : |
| FAVOURITE PART : |
| RATING FROM 1 TO 10 : |
| VOUCHER NO : MEUQ0COG |

THIS VOUCHER ENTITLES YOU TO ONE:

ROUGH SEX SESSION

SEX VOUCHER

REDEEMABLE ANYTIME
NO EXPIRY

VOUCHER NO : MEUQ0COG

| DATE REDEEMED : |
| FAVOURITE PART : |
| RATING FROM 1 TO 10 : |
| VOUCHER NO : D4PV41UD |

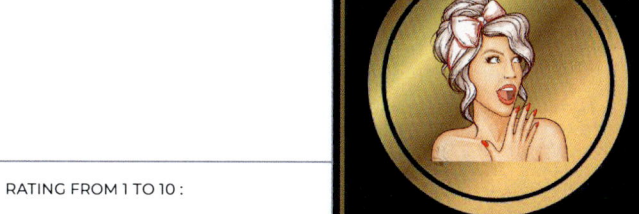

THIS VOUCHER ENTITLES YOU TO ONE:

WHEN I LEAST EXPECT IT, UNDRESS ME AND FUCK ME FROM BEHIND

SEX VOUCHER

REDEEMABLE ANYTIME
NO EXPIRY

VOUCHER NO : D4PV41UD

Terms & Conditions
Tease her by fucking her with the head of your cock only for as long possible.
When she has begged enough, you can deliver the rest.

Terms & Conditions
Agree on a safe word beforehand.
Be more forceful with each other than you normally would.
Think - Choking, slapping, pushing and biting.

Terms & Conditions
Your partner must complete this within 24 hours of the voucher being presented.
Help him out by wearing something with "easy access"

DATE REDEEMED :

FAVOURITE PART :

RATING FROM 1 TO 10 :

VOUCHER NO : **DNEW0RU8**

THIS VOUCHER ENTITLES YOU TO ONE:

ANAL PLAY

REDEEMABLE ANYTIME

NO EXPIRY

SEX VOUCHER

VOUCHER NO : DNEW0RU8

✂ -

DATE REDEEMED :

FAVOURITE PART :

RATING FROM 1 TO 10 :

VOUCHER NO : **2C4MBQPW**

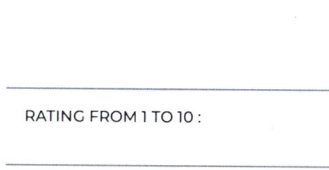

THIS VOUCHER ENTITLES YOU TO ONE:

SUCTION DILDO THREESOME

REDEEMABLE ANYTIME

NO EXPIRY

SEX VOUCHER

VOUCHER NO : 2C4MBQPW

✂ -

DATE REDEEMED :

FAVOURITE PART :

RATING FROM 1 TO 10 :

VOUCHER NO : **R2RLHFOR**

THIS VOUCHER ENTITLES YOU TO ONE:

SEXUAL ROAD TRIP

REDEEMABLE ANYTIME

NO EXPIRY

SEX VOUCHER

VOUCHER NO : R2RLHFOR

Terms & Conditions
Explore her anal playground.
Use fingers, your tongue, lube, toys, your cock, or all if she agrees.

Terms & Conditions
Buy a suction dildo and use it to have a pretend threesome.
Stick the dildo to a hard surface.
She can fuck the dildo while sucking your cock and/or suck the dildo whilst you are fucking her.

Terms & Conditions
Plan to go for a long drive at night together.
The destination is not important but avoid motorways.
Rub, grope and play with each other every time you are stopped by traffic lights.
Both wear clothing with "easy access".
Find somewhere discreet to "complete" the challenge or wait until you are home.

DATE REDEEMED :
FAVOURITE PART :
RATING FROM 1 TO 10 :
VOUCHER NO : **XPJ5CUVH**

THIS VOUCHER ENTITLES YOU TO ONE:

WOMAN'S FILM CHOICE

SEX VOUCHER

REDEEMABLE ANYTIME
NO EXPIRY

VOUCHER NO : XPJ5CUVH

DATE REDEEMED :
FAVOURITE PART :
RATING FROM 1 TO 10 :
VOUCHER NO : **NGWNYOVS**

THIS VOUCHER ENTITLES YOU TO ONE:

COMMANDO DATE NIGHT

SEX VOUCHER

REDEEMABLE ANYTIME
NO EXPIRY

VOUCHER NO : NGWNYOVS

DATE REDEEMED :
FAVOURITE PART :
RATING FROM 1 TO 10 :
VOUCHER NO : **Q8X8AMHR**

THIS VOUCHER ENTITLES YOU TO ONE:

SHE'S THE BOSS EXPERIENCE

SEX VOUCHER

REDEEMABLE ANYTIME
NO EXPIRY

VOUCHER NO : Q8X8AMHR

Terms & Conditions
The lady gets to choose an erotic/porn film for you both to watch together, tonight.

Terms & Conditions
Go out for a date night together.
Wear a skirt or a short dress with no underwear.
Tease him and occasionally, let his hands wander if he is a good boy.

Terms & Conditions
Tonight the lady is in charge! Be very strict.
Both agree on a start time, from that moment forward he must do anything she requests.
Get creative - Tell him to drop and give you 20 press ups, order him to get naked or to get on his knees, etc.

DATE REDEEMED :	
FAVOURITE PART :	
RATING FROM 1 TO 10 :	
VOUCHER NO : **40H1W18V**	

THIS VOUCHER ENTITLES YOU TO ONE:

AGREE ON A NEW SEX TOY TO BUY

REDEEMABLE ANYTIME

NO EXPIRY

SEX VOUCHER

VOUCHER NO : 40H1W18V

DATE REDEEMED :	
FAVOURITE PART :	
RATING FROM 1 TO 10 :	
VOUCHER NO : **PLE8NBBD**	

THIS VOUCHER ENTITLES YOU TO ONE:

EVENING OF STRIP POKER

REDEEMABLE ANYTIME

NO EXPIRY

SEX VOUCHER

VOUCHER NO : PLE8NBBD

DATE REDEEMED :	
FAVOURITE PART :	
RATING FROM 1 TO 10 :	
VOUCHER NO : **9UBURUXV**	

THIS VOUCHER ENTITLES YOU TO ONE:

ADVERTS ARE THE BEST PART

REDEEMABLE ANYTIME

NO EXPIRY

SEX VOUCHER

VOUCHER NO : 9UBURUXV

Terms & Conditions
Sit down together and choose a new sex toy that you would both like to try.
Use the new toy within 48 hours of receiving it.

Terms & Conditions
Start the game fully dressed with the same amount of clothing items.
Agree on the rules beforehand.
Eg; If you lose two hands in a row, you have to remove an item of clothing.
You can play any game you wish if poker is not for you.

Terms & Conditions
Whoever presents this voucher is entitled to receive.
For one film or TV show - Your partner must sexually tease you every time there is an ad break and stop when they finish each time.

DATE REDEEMED :	
FAVOURITE PART :	
RATING FROM 1 TO 10 :	
VOUCHER NO : **VA03SOR9**	

THIS VOUCHER ENTITLES YOU TO ONE:

CUM ON ANY BODY PART YOU CHOOSE

SEX VOUCHER

REDEEMABLE ANYTIME
NO EXPIRY

VOUCHER NO : VA03SOR9

DATE REDEEMED :	
FAVOURITE PART :	
RATING FROM 1 TO 10 :	
VOUCHER NO : **HIUF2R4V**	

THIS VOUCHER ENTITLES YOU TO ONE:

CUM ON ANY BODY PART YOU CHOOSE

SEX VOUCHER

REDEEMABLE ANYTIME
NO EXPIRY

VOUCHER NO : HIUF2R4V

DATE REDEEMED :	
FAVOURITE PART :	
RATING FROM 1 TO 10 :	
VOUCHER NO : **ZW6IS6V0**	

THIS VOUCHER ENTITLES YOU TO ONE:

BUY ME SEXY OUTFIT THAT YOU WANT TO FUCK ME IN

SEX VOUCHER

REDEEMABLE ANYTIME
NO EXPIRY

VOUCHER NO : ZW6IS6V0

Terms & Conditions
He can choose to cum anywhere he desires.

Terms & Conditions
He can choose to cum anywhere he desires.

Terms & Conditions
Buy a sexy outfit for your partner to wear.
Have some fun taking it off.
Must be completed within one week of redemption.

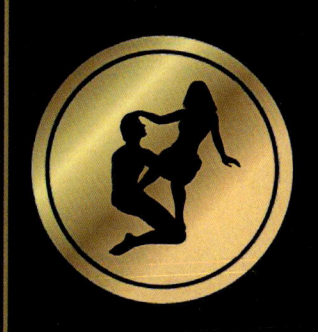

DATE REDEEMED :	
FAVOURITE PART :	**THIS VOUCHER ENTITLES YOU TO ONE:**
	BLINDFOLDED TASTE SESSION
RATING FROM 1 TO 10 :	SEX VOUCHER
VOUCHER NO : **8FCCVHRN**	REDEEMABLE ANYTIME — NO EXPIRY
	VOUCHER NO : 8FCCVHRN

✂ -

DATE REDEEMED :	
FAVOURITE PART :	**THIS VOUCHER ENTITLES YOU TO ONE:**
	SPONTANEOUS ORAL SEX SESSION
RATING FROM 1 TO 10 :	SEX VOUCHER
VOUCHER NO : **GJO9LI97**	REDEEMABLE ANYTIME — NO EXPIRY
	VOUCHER NO : GJO9LI97

✂ -

DATE REDEEMED :	
FAVOURITE PART :	**THIS VOUCHER ENTITLES YOU TO ONE:**
	SPONTANEOUS ORAL SEX SESSION
RATING FROM 1 TO 10 :	SEX VOUCHER
VOUCHER NO : **O4ELSSNB**	REDEEMABLE ANYTIME — NO EXPIRY
	VOUCHER NO : O4ELSSNB

Terms & Conditions
Blindfold your partner, she must lick, suck, nibble anything that is put in front of her.
Use different foods, objects and yourself :)

Terms & Conditions
Either one of you can redeem this voucher.
The person who chooses this voucher is entitled to receive oral sex,
when they least expect it.
The act must be completed within 24 hours of redemption.

Terms & Conditions
Either one of you can redeem this voucher.
The person who chooses this voucher is entitled to receive oral sex,
when they least expect it.
The act must be completed within 24 hours of redemption.

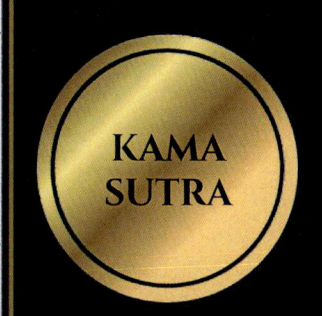

Voucher 1 (stub):
- DATE REDEEMED :
- FAVOURITE PART :
- RATING FROM 1 TO 10 :
- VOUCHER NO : **MK2Z1OSH**

KAMA SUTRA

THIS VOUCHER ENTITLES YOU TO ONE:

TRY A NEW SEX POSITION

SEX VOUCHER

REDEEMABLE ANYTIME

NO EXPIRY

VOUCHER NO : MK2Z1OSH

Voucher 2 (stub):
- DATE REDEEMED :
- FAVOURITE PART :
- RATING FROM 1 TO 10 :
- VOUCHER NO : **EREQX91M**

KAMA SUTRA

THIS VOUCHER ENTITLES YOU TO ONE:

TRY A NEW SEX POSITION

SEX VOUCHER

REDEEMABLE ANYTIME

NO EXPIRY

VOUCHER NO : EREQX91M

Voucher 3 (stub):
- DATE REDEEMED :
- FAVOURITE PART :
- RATING FROM 1 TO 10 :
- VOUCHER NO : **L413GXD9**

THIS VOUCHER ENTITLES YOU TO ONE:

PICK THE BEST MIRROR IN THE HOUSE AND HAVE SEX IN FRONT OF IT

SEX VOUCHER

REDEEMABLE ANYTIME

NO EXPIRY

VOUCHER NO : L413GXD9

Terms & Conditions
The person that redeems this voucher can choose a sex postion
that you have never tried together.
Google "kama sutra" to get some ideas.

Terms & Conditions
The person that redeems this voucher can choose a sex postion
that you have never tried together.
Google "kama sutra" to get some ideas.

Terms & Conditions
Pick the best mirror in the house and have sex in front of it.
This way you can both see things from angles you normally wouldn't.

| DATE REDEEMED : |
| FAVOURITE PART : |
| RATING FROM 1 TO 10 : |
| VOUCHER NO : 800C1N4V |

THIS VOUCHER ENTITLES YOU TO ONE:

WHOEVER MOANS FIRST, LOSES

REDEEMABLE ANYTIME
NO EXPIRY

SEX VOUCHER

VOUCHER NO : 800C1N4V

| DATE REDEEMED : |
| FAVOURITE PART : |
| RATING FROM 1 TO 10 : |
| VOUCHER NO : TQA8ZMB1 |

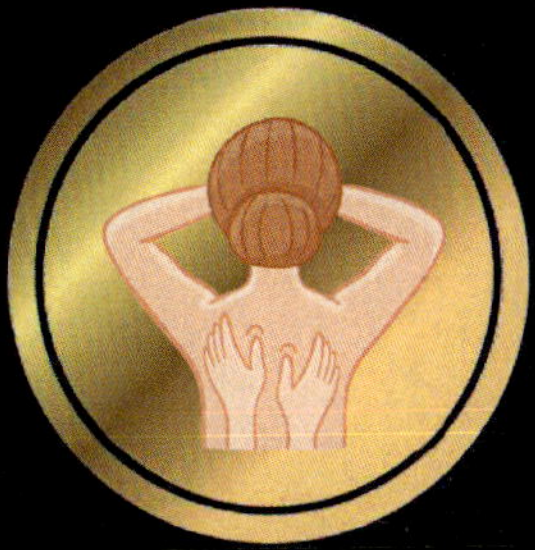

THIS VOUCHER ENTITLES YOU TO ONE:

FULL BODY OIL MASSAGE

REDEEMABLE ANYTIME
NO EXPIRY

SEX VOUCHER

VOUCHER NO : TQA8ZMB1

| DATE REDEEMED : |
| FAVOURITE PART : |
| RATING FROM 1 TO 10 : |
| VOUCHER NO : 6OO22O1F |

THIS VOUCHER ENTITLES YOU TO ONE:

FULL BODY OIL MASSAGE

REDEEMABLE ANYTIME
NO EXPIRY

SEX VOUCHER

VOUCHER NO : 6OO22O1F

Terms & Conditions

Agree on a starting time, from this point onwards try your best to stay silent.
You goal is to make your partner moan.
No tickling or other cheating tactics.
Whoever moans first loses and has to give their partner oral sex the next day.

Terms & Conditions

The person that redeems this voucher will receive a full body oil massage.
Both of you should be naked.

Terms & Conditions

The person that redeems this voucher will receive a full body oil massage.
Both of you should be naked.

DATE REDEEMED :	
FAVOURITE PART :	
RATING FROM 1 TO 10 :	
VOUCHER NO : **23TTTG9G**	

THIS VOUCHER ENTITLES YOU TO ONE:

NO HANDS ALLOWED SEX SESSION

SEX VOUCHER

REDEEMABLE ANYTIME
NO EXPIRY

VOUCHER NO : 23TTTG9G

DATE REDEEMED :	
FAVOURITE PART :	
RATING FROM 1 TO 10 :	
VOUCHER NO : **EAYGHKNS**	

THIS VOUCHER ENTITLES YOU TO ONE:

NO HANDS ALLOWED SEX SESSION

SEX VOUCHER

REDEEMABLE ANYTIME
NO EXPIRY

VOUCHER NO : EAYGHKNS

DATE REDEEMED :	
FAVOURITE PART :	
RATING FROM 1 TO 10 :	
VOUCHER NO : **CBJBRO52**	

THIS VOUCHER ENTITLES YOU TO ONE:

DAY OF NAUGHTY PICTURES

SEX VOUCHER

REDEEMABLE ANYTIME
NO EXPIRY

VOUCHER NO : CBJBRO52

Terms & Conditions
Both get naked.
You are now forbidden to touch each other with your hands. (Anything else goes)

Terms & Conditions
Both get naked.
You are now forbidden to touch each other with your hands. (Anything else goes)

Terms & Conditions
Whoever redeems this voucher is entitled to receive naughty pictures from their partner.
Aim to do this while you are away from each other.
Eg; She sends pictures while he is at work.

DATE REDEEMED :
FAVOURITE PART :
RATING FROM 1 TO 10 :
VOUCHER NO : **WPB6GRLH**

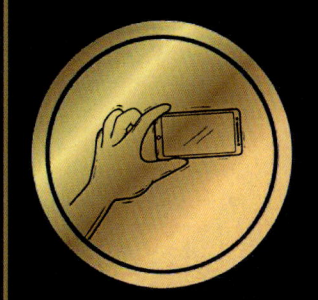

THIS VOUCHER ENTITLES YOU TO ONE:

DAY OF NAUGHTY PICTURES

REDEEMABLE ANYTIME — NO EXPIRY

SEX VOUCHER

VOUCHER NO : WPB6GRLH

DATE REDEEMED :
FAVOURITE PART :
RATING FROM 1 TO 10 :
VOUCHER NO : **1DDBLH9Z**

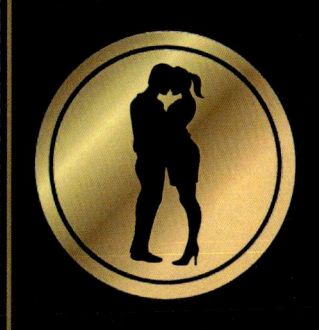

THIS VOUCHER ENTITLES YOU TO ONE:

RISKY SEX OUTSIDE

REDEEMABLE ANYTIME — NO EXPIRY

SEX VOUCHER

VOUCHER NO : 1DDBLH9Z

DATE REDEEMED :
FAVOURITE PART :
RATING FROM 1 TO 10 :
VOUCHER NO : **DLNRK61C**

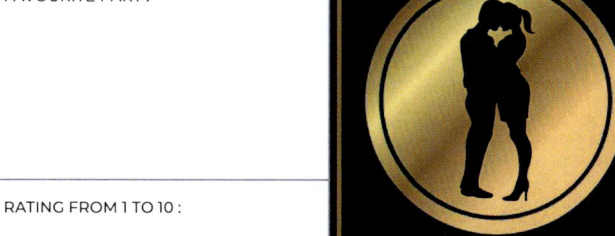

THIS VOUCHER ENTITLES YOU TO ONE:

RISKY SEX OUTSIDE

REDEEMABLE ANYTIME — NO EXPIRY

SEX VOUCHER

VOUCHER NO : DLNRK61C

Terms & Conditions
hoever redeems this voucher is entitled to receive naughty pictures from their partner.
Aim to do this while you are away from each other.
Eg; She sends pictures while he is at work.

Terms & Conditions
Find somewhere outside to get naughty.
Eg; Forest, Car park, Garden, Changing room, etc.

Terms & Conditions
Find somewhere outside to get naughty.
Eg; Forest, Car park, Garden, Changing room, etc.

DATE REDEEMED :	
FAVOURITE PART :	
RATING FROM 1 TO 10 :	
VOUCHER NO : **2BRUM5NB**	

THIS VOUCHER ENTITLES YOU TO ONE:

I WANT TO USE YOUR FACE LIKE A SEAT

SEX VOUCHER

REDEEMABLE ANYTIME

NO EXPIRY

VOUCHER NO : 2BRUM5NB

DATE REDEEMED :	
FAVOURITE PART :	
RATING FROM 1 TO 10 :	
VOUCHER NO : **GGSUJ5X2**	

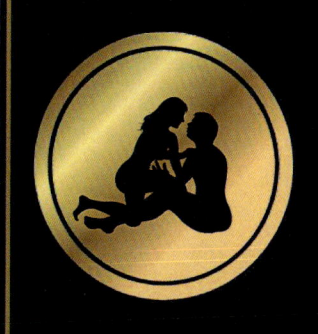

THIS VOUCHER ENTITLES YOU TO ONE:

I WANT TO USE YOUR FACE LIKE A SEAT

SEX VOUCHER

REDEEMABLE ANYTIME

NO EXPIRY

VOUCHER NO : GGSUJ5X2

DATE REDEEMED :	
FAVOURITE PART :	
RATING FROM 1 TO 10 :	
VOUCHER NO : **GNNQ4VY3**	

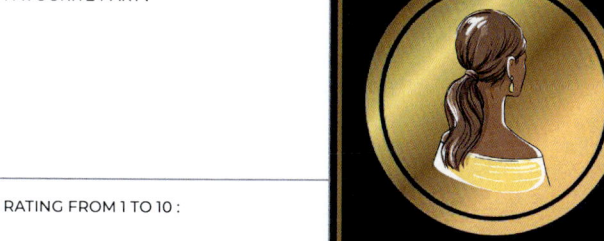

THIS VOUCHER ENTITLES YOU TO ONE:

PLAY WITH MY HAIR FOR 20 MINUTES, THEN TIE IT UP SO I CAN SUCK YOUR COCK

SEX VOUCHER

REDEEMABLE ANYTIME

NO EXPIRY

VOUCHER NO : GNNQ4VY3

Terms & Conditions
Your partner must lay on his back.
He is forbidden to move anything apart from his tongue.
Now ride his face however you desire.

Terms & Conditions
Your partner must lay on his back.
He is forbidden to move anything apart from his tongue.
Now ride his face however you desire.

Terms & Conditions
Get him to brush or play with your hair for 20 minutes.
Then with your hair tied up, suck his cock.

DATE REDEEMED :	
FAVOURITE PART :	
RATING FROM 1 TO 10 :	
VOUCHER NO : **53W700I2**	

THIS VOUCHER ENTITLES YOU TO ONE:

LISTEN TO AN EROTIC AUDIO BOOK TOGETHER

SEX VOUCHER

REDEEMABLE ANYTIME

NO EXPIRY

VOUCHER NO : 53W700I2

DATE REDEEMED :	
FAVOURITE PART :	
RATING FROM 1 TO 10 :	
VOUCHER NO : **P639GW5A**	

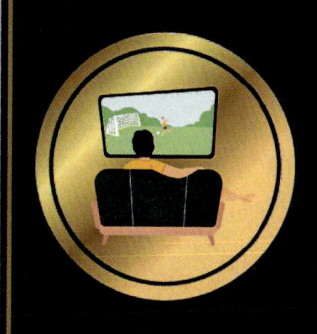

THIS VOUCHER ENTITLES YOU TO ONE:

BLOWJOB WHILE WATCHING SPORTS

SEX VOUCHER

REDEEMABLE ANYTIME

NO EXPIRY

VOUCHER NO : P639GW5A

DATE REDEEMED :	
FAVOURITE PART :	
RATING FROM 1 TO 10 :	
VOUCHER NO : **4A9KPAU9**	

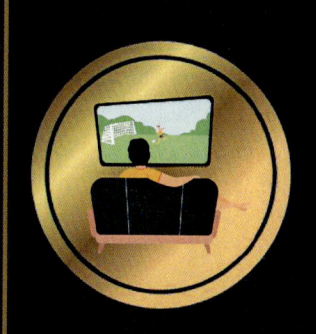

THIS VOUCHER ENTITLES YOU TO ONE:

BLOWJOB WHILE WATCHING SPORTS

SEX VOUCHER

REDEEMABLE ANYTIME

NO EXPIRY

VOUCHER NO : 4A9KPAU9

Terms & Conditions
Choose an erotic audio book together.
Audible offer free trials, they have thousands of steamy erotic novels.
Listen together and see what happens.

Terms & Conditions
He is entitled to receive one blowjob whilst watching sports or his favourite tv show.

Terms & Conditions
He is entitled to receive one blowjob whilst watching sports or his favourite tv show.

DATE REDEEMED :	
FAVOURITE PART :	
RATING FROM 1 TO 10 :	
VOUCHER NO : **S98AZ7D0**	

THIS VOUCHER ENTITLES YOU TO ONE:

BONDAGE SESSION

SEX
VOUCHER

REDEEMABLE ANYTIME

NO EXPIRY

VOUCHER NO : S98AZ7D0

DATE REDEEMED :	
FAVOURITE PART :	
RATING FROM 1 TO 10 :	
VOUCHER NO : **BCYO8E50**	

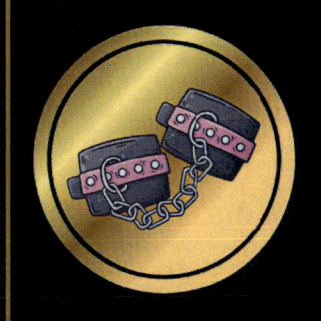

THIS VOUCHER ENTITLES YOU TO ONE:

BONDAGE SESSION

SEX
VOUCHER

REDEEMABLE ANYTIME

NO EXPIRY

VOUCHER NO : BCYO8E50

DATE REDEEMED :	
FAVOURITE PART :	
RATING FROM 1 TO 10 :	
VOUCHER NO : **ALH2MYVD**	

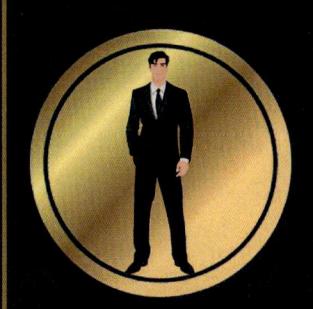

THIS VOUCHER ENTITLES YOU TO ONE:

NIGHT OF ROLEPLAY

SEX
VOUCHER

REDEEMABLE ANYTIME

NO EXPIRY

VOUCHER NO : ALH2MYVD

Terms & Conditions
Whoever redeems this voucher can choose to be tied up or be in control.
Whoever is in control has the power to do anything sexual they want to the other.

Terms & Conditions
Whoever redeems this voucher can choose to be tied up or be in control.
Whoever is in control has the power to do anything sexual they want to the other.

Terms & Conditions
Choose a scenario together eg; strangers at a bar, teacher and student, handyman coming to fix something, taxi driver etc, and then make it happen.

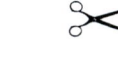

DATE REDEEMED :	
FAVOURITE PART :	
RATING FROM 1 TO 10 :	
VOUCHER NO : **J83VQK3D**	

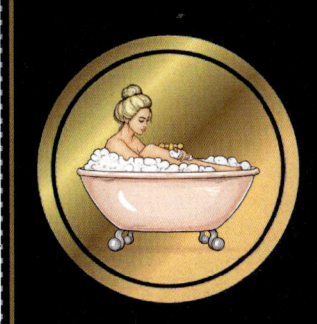

THIS VOUCHER ENTITLES YOU TO ONE:

ROMANTIC BATH WITH A HAPPY ENDING

SEX VOUCHER

REDEEMABLE ANYTIME
NO EXPIRY

VOUCHER NO : J83VQK3D

✂ -

DATE REDEEMED :	
FAVOURITE PART :	
RATING FROM 1 TO 10 :	
VOUCHER NO : **JQ5IB9YL**	

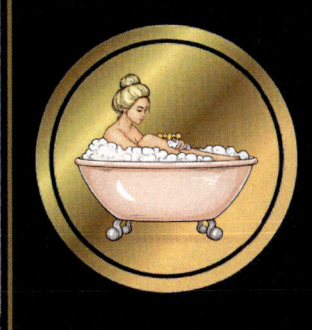

THIS VOUCHER ENTITLES YOU TO ONE:

ROMANTIC BATH WITH A HAPPY ENDING

SEX VOUCHER

REDEEMABLE ANYTIME
NO EXPIRY

VOUCHER NO : JQ5IB9YL

✂ -

DATE REDEEMED :	
FAVOURITE PART :	
RATING FROM 1 TO 10 :	
VOUCHER NO : **VBEHDQIC**	

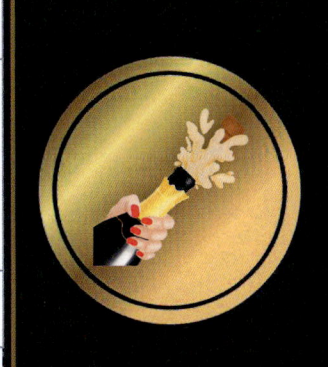

THIS VOUCHER ENTITLES YOU TO ONE:

TEASING THIGH MASSAGE

SEX VOUCHER

REDEEMABLE ANYTIME
NO EXPIRY

VOUCHER NO : VBEHDQIC

Terms & Conditions
Run her a romantic bath with candles and bubbles.
Let her relax for 20 minutes then come back and make her cum.

Terms & Conditions
Run her a romantic bath with candles and bubbles.
Let her relax for 20 minutes then come back and make her cum.

Terms & Conditions
While you are sitting on the bed or sofa, she must give you a thigh massage.
Teasing around your cock, brushing past it and licking around it, until she chooses to give into your pleasure.

DATE REDEEMED :	
FAVOURITE PART :	
RATING FROM 1 TO 10 :	
VOUCHER NO : **12TCFA8B**	

THIS VOUCHER ENTITLES YOU TO ONE:

TEASING THIGH MASSAGE

SEX VOUCHER

REDEEMABLE ANYTIME

NO EXPIRY

VOUCHER NO : 12TCFA8B

DATE REDEEMED :	
FAVOURITE PART :	
RATING FROM 1 TO 10 :	
VOUCHER NO : **DUOOVFUT**	

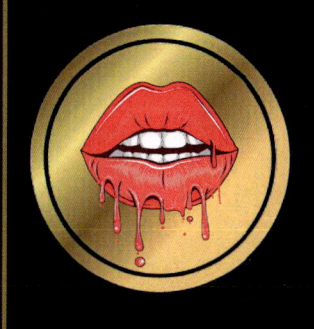

THIS VOUCHER ENTITLES YOU TO ONE:

SUPER SLOPPY BLOWJOB

SEX VOUCHER

REDEEMABLE ANYTIME

NO EXPIRY

VOUCHER NO : DUOOVFUT

DATE REDEEMED :	
FAVOURITE PART :	
RATING FROM 1 TO 10 :	
VOUCHER NO : **0ABBV340**	

THIS VOUCHER ENTITLES YOU TO ONE:

WETTER THAN AN OTTER'S POCKET

SEX VOUCHER

REDEEMABLE ANYTIME

NO EXPIRY

VOUCHER NO : 0ABBV340

Terms & Conditions
While you are sitting on the bed or sofa, he must give you a thigh massage.
Teasing around your pussy, brushing past it and licking around it, until he chooses
to give into your pleasure.

Terms & Conditions
Give your partner the wettest blowjob ever.
The wetter and sloppier the better.

Terms & Conditions
Go down on your partner.
Spit all over her pussy and make her the wettest she has ever been.
The wetter and sloppier the better.

DATE REDEEMED :	
FAVOURITE PART :	
RATING FROM 1 TO 10 :	
VOUCHER NO : **VYVQMYNS**	

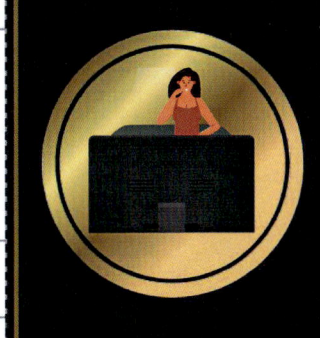

THIS VOUCHER ENTITLES YOU TO ONE:

GO DOWN ON ME WHILE I'M WATCHING MY FAVOURITE SHOW

REDEEMABLE ANYTIME
NO EXPIRY

SEX VOUCHER

VOUCHER NO : VYVQMYNS

DATE REDEEMED :	
FAVOURITE PART :	
RATING FROM 1 TO 10 :	
VOUCHER NO : **VZGTRX8L**	

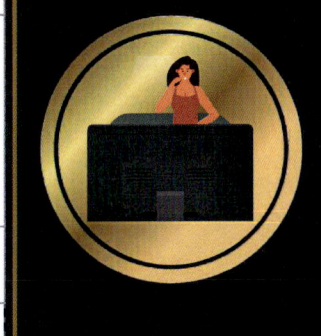

THIS VOUCHER ENTITLES YOU TO ONE:

GO DOWN ON ME WHILE I'M WATCHING MY FAVOURITE SHOW

REDEEMABLE ANYTIME
NO EXPIRY

SEX VOUCHER

VOUCHER NO : VZGTRX8L

DATE REDEEMED :	
FAVOURITE PART :	
RATING FROM 1 TO 10 :	
VOUCHER NO : **JCDP6B43**	

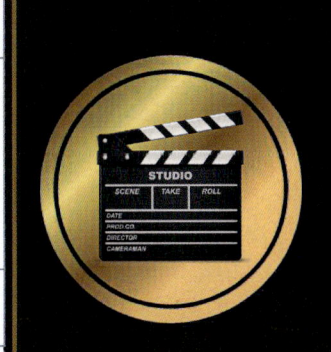

THIS VOUCHER ENTITLES YOU TO ONE:

MAKE A SEX TAPE

REDEEMABLE ANYTIME
NO EXPIRY

SEX VOUCHER

VOUCHER NO : JCDP6B43

Terms & Conditions
After she has redeemed this voucher, you have to go down on her.
Give your man a start signal by saying "I love this show"
His mission is to try and distract you as much as possible.
Your challenge is to keep focused on the TV.

Terms & Conditions
After she has redeemed this voucher, you have to go down on her.
Give your man a start signal by saying "I love this show"
His mission is to try and distract you as much as possible.
Your challenge is to keep focused on the TV.

Terms & Conditions
Record yourselves having sex or performing oral.
Watch the video back together within a week to get you in the mood again.

DATE REDEEMED :	
FAVOURITE PART :	
RATING FROM 1 TO 10 :	
VOUCHER NO : **JQ5YYHBF**	

THIS VOUCHER ENTITLES YOU TO ONE:

SEX RIGHT HERE, RIGHT NOW

REDEEMABLE ANYTIME
NO EXPIRY

SEX VOUCHER

VOUCHER NO : JQ5YYHBF

DATE REDEEMED :	
FAVOURITE PART :	
RATING FROM 1 TO 10 :	
VOUCHER NO : **7IZTMQ7M**	

THIS VOUCHER ENTITLES YOU TO ONE:

MAKE A SEX PLAYLIST

REDEEMABLE ANYTIME
NO EXPIRY

SEX VOUCHER

VOUCHER NO : 7IZTMQ7M

DATE REDEEMED :	
FAVOURITE PART :	
RATING FROM 1 TO 10 :	
VOUCHER NO : **P6Q23U1G**	

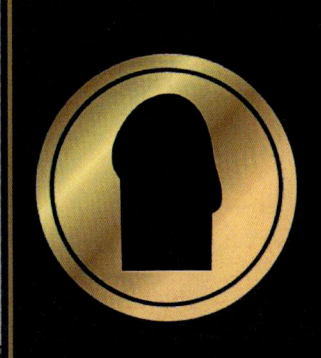

THIS VOUCHER ENTITLES YOU TO ONE:

MAKE HIM BEG BLOWJOB

REDEEMABLE ANYTIME
NO EXPIRY

SEX VOUCHER

VOUCHER NO : P6Q23U1G

Terms & Conditions
When this voucher is presented, you should have sex immediately.

Terms & Conditions
Choose 5 sexy and seductive songs each.
Add them all to a playlist.
Make love while you listen to them.

Terms & Conditions
Give your man a blowjob. However, you must tease him for as long as possible.
You can only suck the head of his cock and no further.
You can lick as much as you want.
When you feel like he has begged enough, suck the soul out of him.

DATE REDEEMED :	
FAVOURITE PART :	
RATING FROM 1 TO 10 :	
VOUCHER NO : **GX53UMPY**	

THIS VOUCHER ENTITLES YOU TO ONE:

CUM PLAY WITH ME

REDEEMABLE ANYTIME
NO EXPIRY

SEX VOUCHER

VOUCHER NO : GX53UMPY

DATE REDEEMED :	
FAVOURITE PART :	
RATING FROM 1 TO 10 :	
VOUCHER NO : **TBB43REB**	

THIS VOUCHER ENTITLES YOU TO ONE:

69 ER

REDEEMABLE ANYTIME
NO EXPIRY

SEX VOUCHER

VOUCHER NO : TBB43REB

DATE REDEEMED :	
FAVOURITE PART :	
RATING FROM 1 TO 10 :	
VOUCHER NO : **EVDT80GJ**	

THIS VOUCHER ENTITLES YOU TO ONE:

69 ER

REDEEMABLE ANYTIME
NO EXPIRY

SEX VOUCHER

VOUCHER NO : EVDT80GJ

Terms & Conditions
masterbate next to, or opposite each other until you cum. (opposite works best)
You can not touch each other.

Terms & Conditions
This voucher is pretty straight forward.
However, mix the position up a bit, try it on your sides or him on top.

Terms & Conditions
This voucher is pretty straight forward.
However, mix the position up a bit, try it on your sides or him on top.

DATE REDEEMED :
FAVOURITE PART :
RATING FROM 1 TO 10 :
VOUCHER NO : **0ZGQSDXO**

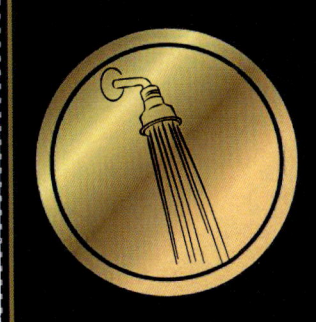

THIS VOUCHER ENTITLES YOU TO ONE:

STEAMY SHOWER TOGETHER

REDEEMABLE ANYTIME
NO EXPIRY

SEX VOUCHER

VOUCHER NO : 0ZGQSDXO

DATE REDEEMED :
FAVOURITE PART :
RATING FROM 1 TO 10 :
VOUCHER NO : **3DRP7PI5**

THIS VOUCHER ENTITLES YOU TO ONE:

STEAMY SHOWER TOGETHER

REDEEMABLE ANYTIME
NO EXPIRY

SEX VOUCHER

VOUCHER NO : 3DRP7PI5

DATE REDEEMED :
FAVOURITE PART :
RATING FROM 1 TO 10 :
VOUCHER NO : **TD7PHAFT**

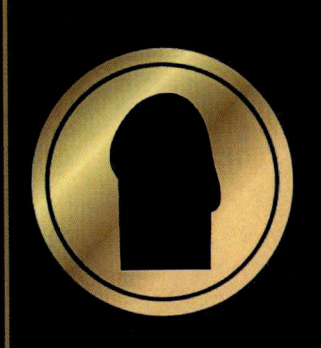

THIS VOUCHER ENTITLES YOU TO ONE:

JUST THE TIP

REDEEMABLE ANYTIME
NO EXPIRY

SEX VOUCHER

VOUCHER NO : TD7PHAFT

Terms & Conditions
Take a shower together.
Wash each other thoroughly until you are clean, then get filthy.

Terms & Conditions
Take a shower together.
Wash each other thoroughly until you are clean, then get yourselves dirty ;)

Terms & Conditions
Tease her by fucking her with the head of your cock only for as long possible.
When she has begged enough, you can deliver the rest.

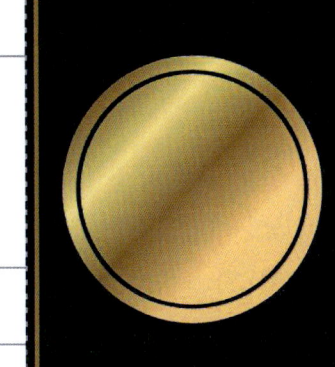

DATE REDEEMED :

FAVOURITE PART :

RATING FROM 1 TO 10 :

VOUCHER NO : **B8PM1EIT**

THIS VOUCHER ENTITLES YOU TO ONE:

SEX VOUCHER

REDEEMABLE ANYTIME
NO EXPIRY

VOUCHER NO : B8PM1EIT

DATE REDEEMED :

FAVOURITE PART :

RATING FROM 1 TO 10 :

VOUCHER NO : **4GCXMM4Z**

THIS VOUCHER ENTITLES YOU TO ONE:

SEX VOUCHER

REDEEMABLE ANYTIME
NO EXPIRY

VOUCHER NO : 4GCXMM4Z

DATE REDEEMED :

FAVOURITE PART :

RATING FROM 1 TO 10 :

VOUCHER NO : **OP36TSAJ**

THIS VOUCHER ENTITLES YOU TO ONE:

SEX VOUCHER

REDEEMABLE ANYTIME
NO EXPIRY

VOUCHER NO : OP36TSAJ

Terms & Conditions
You are in control of the rules now.

Terms & Conditions
You are in control of the rules now.

Terms & Conditions
You are in control of the rules now.

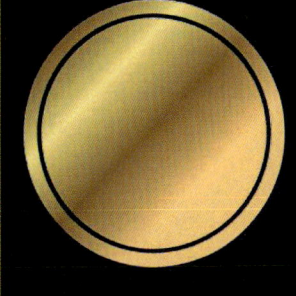

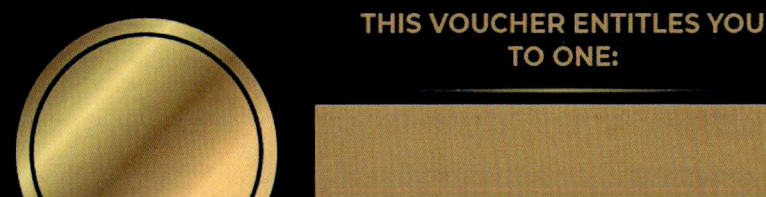

DATE REDEEMED :

FAVOURITE PART :

RATING FROM 1 TO 10 :

VOUCHER NO : **RTMTP4ZM**

THIS VOUCHER ENTITLES YOU TO ONE:

SEX VOUCHER

REDEEMABLE ANYTIME

NO EXPIRY

VOUCHER NO : RTMTP4ZM

DATE REDEEMED :

FAVOURITE PART :

RATING FROM 1 TO 10 :

VOUCHER NO : **INK5VWND**

THIS VOUCHER ENTITLES YOU TO ONE:

SEX VOUCHER

REDEEMABLE ANYTIME

NO EXPIRY

VOUCHER NO : INK5VWND

DATE REDEEMED :

FAVOURITE PART :

RATING FROM 1 TO 10 :

VOUCHER NO : **UD7QWGPT**

THIS VOUCHER ENTITLES YOU TO ONE:

SEX VOUCHER

REDEEMABLE ANYTIME

NO EXPIRY

VOUCHER NO : UD7QWGPT

Terms & Conditions
You are in control of the rules now.

Terms & Conditions
You are in control of the rules now.

Terms & Conditions
You are in control of the rules now.

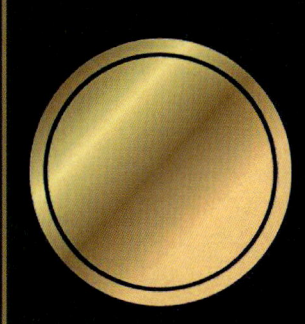

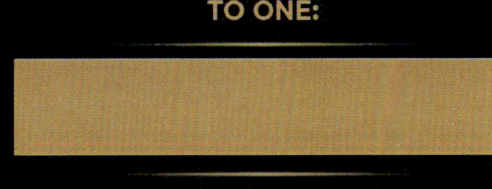

DATE REDEEMED :	
FAVOURITE PART :	
RATING FROM 1 TO 10 :	
VOUCHER NO : **C4WTRHKE**	

THIS VOUCHER ENTITLES YOU TO ONE:

SEX VOUCHER

REDEEMABLE ANYTIME
NO EXPIRY

VOUCHER NO : C4WTRHKE

✂ -

DATE REDEEMED :	
FAVOURITE PART :	
RATING FROM 1 TO 10 :	
VOUCHER NO : **UCM923T8**	

THIS VOUCHER ENTITLES YOU TO ONE:

SEX VOUCHER

REDEEMABLE ANYTIME
NO EXPIRY

VOUCHER NO : UCM923T8

✂ -

DATE REDEEMED :	
FAVOURITE PART :	
RATING FROM 1 TO 10 :	
VOUCHER NO : **UNLTTPJ4**	

THIS VOUCHER ENTITLES YOU TO ONE:

SEX VOUCHER

REDEEMABLE ANYTIME
NO EXPIRY

VOUCHER NO : UNLTTPJ4

Terms & Conditions
You are in control of the rules now.

Terms & Conditions
You are in control of the rules now.

Terms & Conditions
You are in control of the rules now.

DATE REDEEMED :

FAVOURITE PART :

RATING FROM 1 TO 10 :

VOUCHER NO : **D1GGVRZ5**

THIS VOUCHER ENTITLES YOU TO ONE:

SEX VOUCHER

REDEEMABLE ANYTIME

NO EXPIRY

VOUCHER NO : D1GGVRZ5

✂ -

DATE REDEEMED :

FAVOURITE PART :

RATING FROM 1 TO 10 :

VOUCHER NO : **O9YTU87Y**

THIS VOUCHER ENTITLES YOU TO ONE:

SEX VOUCHER

REDEEMABLE ANYTIME

NO EXPIRY

VOUCHER NO : O9YTU87Y

✂ -

DATE REDEEMED :

FAVOURITE PART :

RATING FROM 1 TO 10 :

VOUCHER NO : **DKKQJGPZ**

THIS VOUCHER ENTITLES YOU TO ONE:

SEX VOUCHER

REDEEMABLE ANYTIME

NO EXPIRY

VOUCHER NO : DKKQJGPZ

Terms & Conditions
You are in control of the rules now.

Terms & Conditions
You are in control of the rules now.

Terms & Conditions
You are in control of the rules now.

Manufactured by Amazon.ca
Acheson, AB